A LOST MALTI

GARDEN

John Hookham Frere's
Masterpiece

Josephine Tyndale-Biscoe

A LOST MALTESE GARDEN

John Hookham Frere's Masterpiece

Josephine Tyndale-Biscoe

BIRCHQUEST

A LOST MALTESE GARDEN
John Hookham Frere's Masterpiece

ISBN 978-0-9563849-0-4

Published by
Birchquest Ltd.
Cedar Croft
Sunny Way, Bosham,
West Sussex PO18 8HQ

A CIP catalogue record of this book
can be obtained from the British Library.

Book designed by Michael Walsh at
THE BETTER BOOK COMPANY

Printed by
ASHFORD COLOUR PRESS
Unit 600 Fareham Reach
Fareham Road
Gosport
Hants PO13 0FW

CONTENTS

FOREWORD

This is the story of a childhood fascination with a lost garden, and the remarkable English gentleman scholar who lovingly created it out of a rocky slope, which ran down to the creek in Pietà. As a child, Jo Tyndale-Biscoe must have heard her grandmother tell a story of a fabulous garden overlooking the quarantine harbour of Marsamuxetto in the island of Malta, where she grew up. Her grandmother's grandfather was the wealthy Count Rosario Messina. He had bought the lease of the mansion, known as Villa Frere and its splendid garden, after the death of its former owner the Rt. Hon. John Hookham Frere, the genial Cambridge scholar, diplomat, and poet, who had retired to Malta, and lived on the island for twenty-five years. Frere, a true Englishman, was fond of cultivating his garden and he slowly and painstakingly transformed it into his own personal 'delectable spot', which was eventually to become one of the most beautiful gardens on the island.

This book began as a dream to enter that elusive lost garden, in which her grandmother played as a child. The garden has vanished into the miasma of the past. But in the course of her quest, Jo Tyndale-Biscoe has succeeded in retrieving Villa Frere and its garden from the shades of oblivion, and presenting it to the reader in a charming verbal and visual reconstruction of its pristine glory.

Professor Peter Vassallo
Department of English
University of Malta

Introduction

If you chose to walk along the busy Marina Street in Pietà, you might notice an old house with the name just visible on the front doorway pillars – Villa Frere – but you would not think twice. Then, if you walked up the hill towards St. Luke's Hospital, you would find a road called Hookham Frere Street, and further on you would come to the Hookham Frere Primary School. By now you should be inquisitive, and be wanting to know who Hookham Frere might have been.

Plate 1 Villa Frere in 1907. It is the 3 storey white building in the centre – the gardens extended over the hill behind

I want to take you on an historical journey from 1826 to the present day. My fascination is with the memories of a villa and its garden in Malta, which belonged to a great British scholar and diplomat, the Right Honourable John Hookham Frere. He was one of the most important and influential British personalities to have settled in Malta during the first half of the 19th century. My interest began as a descendant of the family who bought the villa in Malta, after the Hookham Frere family. All my life I had heard of Malta from my grandmother, Dolores Baxter (née Price), as it was her family home.

Chapter 1

Who was John Hookham Frere?

The Right Honourable John Hookham Frere was a remarkable man of his day, and is justly remembered by the people of Malta. He was born in London in 1769 and became a writer and diplomat, scholar, poet and humanitarian. His father, John Frere, came from a cultured Suffolk family. His mother, daughter of John Hookham, a rich London merchant, was known for her poetry. He was educated at Eton College, where he became friends with George Canning, who was to become Foreign Secretary under William Pitt the Younger, and who greatly influenced his later life. After graduating from Caius College, Cambridge in 1792, he entered public service in the Foreign Office under Lord Grenville, and sat from 1796-1802 as Member of Parliament for the borough of West Looe, in Cornwall. From his boyhood he had been an admirer of William Pitt the Younger, and in collaboration with Canning he contributed short burlesque poems to *The Anti-Jacobin*, a satirical Tory journal of the day.

Frere had an interesting diplomatic career, which began in 1800, when he was appointed Envoy Extraordinary and Plenipotentiary to Lisbon. In 1802 he was transferred to Madrid. He was made a member of the Privy Council in 1805, and in 1808 he was again sent to Spain as Plenipotentiary to the Central Junta. The disastrous British retreat from Madrid to Corunna, in which Sir John Moore was killed, reflected badly on Hookham Frere, who had advised the British to withdraw. After public outcry, he was recalled, and his diplomatic life effectively ended at this time. He must have been very dissatisfied with his treatment, as he twice declined a Peerage, and also refused to accept the post of Ambassador in St. Petersburg.

After his marriage in 1816, aged 46, he went to live in Malta in 1821 with his Irish wife, Elizabeth Jemima, Dowager Countess of Errol. In August 1820, Frere had chartered a sailing vessel called "Sicily", commanded by Captain Cupper. They sailed for the Mediterranean, together with Frere's unmarried sister, Susan, and Miss Honoria Blake, a niece of Elizabeth Frere. The voyage took them to Lisbon and then on to the Mediterranean. Frere seems to have been at one time inclined to settle at Palermo, but finally preferred Malta. As he drew his pension from England, he said "he would rather spend his life amongst other British subjects."

JOHN HOOKHAM FRERE
1769 - 1846

Plate 2 – Portrait in Hookham Frere Primary School

Initially, the Frere family lived in Valletta at 176, Casa Correa, in Old Bakery Street. During the hot summer months, they also lived in an unassuming waterside villa in Pietà (see Plate 1) which they bought on a 99 year lease. Here, with very little interruption, he spent the remaining years of his life. Upon arrival in Malta in 1821 in the sailing boat '*Sicily*', and having no further orders, the master of the vessel, Captain Cupper, was free to leave. He made several trips at this time, during the Greek War of Independence, to help the Greek people in their struggle against the Turks in the Gulf of Corinth. On one such visit, he heard of an orphan child who had been rescued from slaughter by a Turkish soldier, and he brought her to the safety of Alexandria, where she was entrusted into the care of another sea-captain and his wife to be taken to Frere in Malta. In due course, they arrived, and the child was taken to the Villa where Elizabeth Frere at once received her into the house, and she was brought up as one of the family. The little girl was then about five years old, and could not manage to tell them anything about herself at all, not even her name. Frere called her Statyra, after the wife of Darius, King of Persia, a famous beauty in her time. He added the surname of Lividostro, after the village where she was found. Captain Cupper describes her as being a 'sweet little brown maid', while a friend who knew her in later years says 'she was a very diminutive old lady, but exceedingly kind and very loveable, being of a very sweet disposition'. In 1835, we know that she married a relative of Elizabeth Frere, Captain William Hope of the 7th Fusiliers, who was stationed with his regiment at Malta. He met her due to a riding accident in Pietà, when his horse fell, causing his leg to be broken. He was carried to the Villa, and remained there until his leg mended. Statyra and Captain Hope fell in love and were married at the Villa, and as guardian to Statyra, Frere would have been proud to give her away on her wedding day. The couple had two daughters, who lived in Malta, and who related this story to my great grandfather, Edward Price.

Chapter 2

The Gardens at Villa Frere

Once Frere and his wife, Elizabeth, had settled in Malta, in 1820, they chose to live in Pietà. They bought various adjoining properties, and the garden eventually covered about 3 acres. Although a local architect was employed, there does not appear to be any studied plan in the design of the gardens. The original land was little more than a bare, rocky hillside sloping down to the sea – a wilderness of walls, prickly pears and Aruba trees. One great advantage that these gardens had, was the fact that they were remarkably sheltered.

Of geological interest is the "dreadful awful hole" mentioned in Edward Price's booklet on Villa Frere. This hole was discovered whilst the kitchen garden was being formed. A large piece of rock, when it was being removed, it was found to rest on a layer of clay about 27 feet long and 15 feet wide. This was used to form good gardening soil. In this digging, many stones were found in the clay, evidently rounded by the action of water. The sides of the rock formed an irregular funnel, suggesting the passage of water to some cavity below. With the hope of finding a water supply for the gardens, work carried on until it reached the sea level, about 60 feet below, when the hole filled with water from the sea.

Plate 3 A well head

Plan of Villa Frere at Pietá

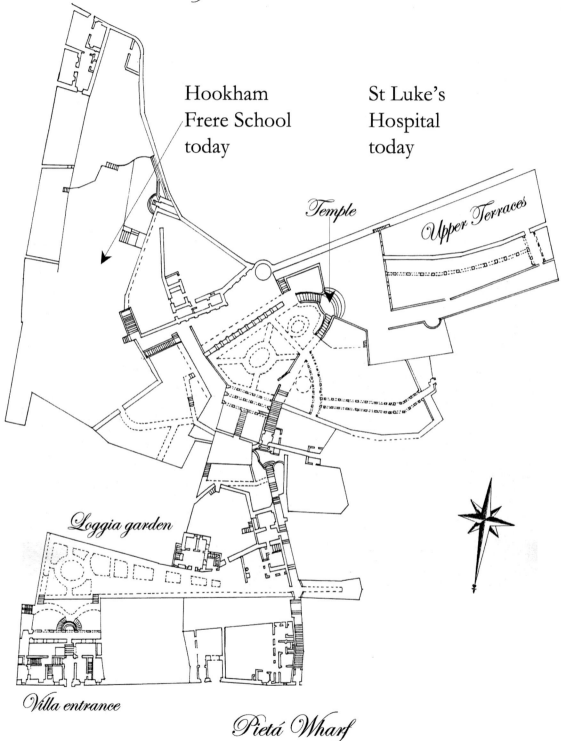

Hookham
Frere School
today

St Luke's
Hospital
today

Temple

Upper Terraces

Loggia garden

Villa entrance

Pietá Wharf

Plate 4 Plan of the Garden

(by permission of Govt. Works Dept., Floriana, Malta)

The land was levelled into many terraces, and on each level there were several water cisterns (possibly as many as 13), to catch water in the winter rains, and to provide irrigation during the dry summertime, all with elaborate carved stone well-heads.

A vast sum of money must have been spent on creating this garden of gardens, which included orange groves, Dutch tulip gardens, flower terraces, a vegetable garden, a Sundial garden, a reed-filled fountain, Pergolas and Terraces, and a large garden temple.

Plate 5 Fountain

(copyright Country Life)

Plate 6 Upper Terrace

Plate 7 The Temple

The temple, or neo-classical gazebo, is the largest building of the old garden still standing. In the words of the famous English landscape and garden designer, Sir Geoffrey Jellicoe, "No Greek building attempted to dominate the landscape". The Greek genius was to collaborate with the landscape in order to discover an inner balance between man and nature. This balance would have been achieved in Frere's garden. It used to stand proudly in the midst of the lush garden foliage, but today it looks sadly out of place behind St.Luke's Hospital buildings, where no-one notices it. But let us stay in the past, when the gardens prospered and were cared for.

Plate 8 The Wall today

The wall at the top of the gardens was built by fitting large blocks of stone together, without the aid of mortar. The wall is 90 feet long, and 13 ft high, and can still be seen today near the ruins of the Temple.

Chapter 3

A Tour of the Gardens

We start at the pillared front door on the waterside villa on Pietà Wharf. It is only one room deep, but has three floors and extensive outbuildings, which once included stabling for horses and carriages. Passing the wrought-iron staircase, and crossing the cool marble floor tiles, you find yourself at the rear of the house on a spacious arcaded loggia – much needed in the Maltese summer.

Plate 9 Loggia

From the loggia, you would see a carpet of bedding plants on the lower gardens, which were re-planted with the changing seasons. Along the path, on your right, there was a small orange grove, before the first flight of steps led you to the terraces above.

Plate 10 Lower Terrace

There were trees everywhere – pines, carobs, cypresses, olives, figs, pomegranates, oaks, oranges, lemons, and tamarind. There was a fine example of Dracena drago (Dragon's Blood tree) a native of the Canary Islands. It was nearly 8m high, 3m in girth, and was 100 years old in 1926.

Plate 11 Dragon's Blood tree

The following description, found in Edward Price's booklet, provides us with an excellent contemporary view of the garden.

"Imagine then, a garden all warmth and sunshine, and beautiful views of the bluest of seas; a garden where, without being actually a maze, everything comes upon you as a surprise; a garden too, filled with beautiful shrubs and lovely freesias, hyacinths, roses and sweetest violets, palms, and other rare plants; a garden with quaintly carved stone benches, and with a dreadful, awful hole in the centre, leading far down through a tunnel into the bowels of the earth, and suggesting terrible deeds of darkness; a garden with its sundial, and its temple, and lovers' nooks, peacocks, gazelles, gold and silver pheasants; a garden such as Doré, and only Doré might have painted! Such is the garden of Villa Frere". (Gustave Doré, was a famous French artist at the time, whose paintings had a dream-like quality.)

Plate 12 The Pergola

Plate 13 Upper terrace

(copyright Country Life)

"The blue waters rippled clear and undefiled, against the white retaining walls of the road, which separated the house from the harbour. The building itself ... extended for some distance along the road at the foot of a rocky hill, rising steeply from the waterside. Behind the house, this steep hill has, with great labour, been converted into a garden. The whole rock, up to the summit, is cut into terraces and platforms, parts of which are filled with earth brought from a considerable distance. Many of the terraces are enclosed by walls, and upon others are double rows of columns supporting trellis work, covered with creepers. The different stages are approached by flights of steps – and the whole hill is excavated into tanks containing a good supply of rain water. The view from the Temple at its summit, is very singular. The garden looks like a collection of sheep-folds, but nothing can be richer than the heavy ornate staircases, temples, seats and benches, lines of arches and balustrades, Gothic and Moorish turrets, and stone well-heads for raising the water from the tanks are carved in the fine white Maltese stone, with bold and flowery patterns in excellent taste. As to the trees and shrubs, all kinds from cedar to the hyssop are there – figs, palms, orange, lemon, tamarind, vine, pomegranate, olive, magnificent geraniums, legions of roses and carnations."

Plate 14 View from Engagement Terrace over Msida Creek
(copyright Country Life)

The upper terraces, known to the Price family as Lover's Walk and Engagement Terrace, with their balustrades and pots, full of flowers, led to the temple at the top of the garden, from which there were extensive views over Msida creek.

Chapter 4

Frere's Life in Malta

Although Frere abstained from politics, he took a deep interest in Maltese affairs. Malta has cause to be very grateful to him, particularly for his support of the impoverished language scholar, Mikiel Anton Vassalli. In 1820 Vassalli returned to Malta from living in France and Spain with his wife and three young sons, and were befriended by the Frere family. In 1795, Vassalli had completed the first Maltese Dictionary, Alphabet and Grammar Book ever to be written down. Until this time, the Maltese language had only been a spoken one. Unfortunately, he could not get them printed in Malta, but with Frere's generous help, the books were sent to England for printing. When Vassalli died, in 1829 there was much strong feeling that he should be honoured fairly. Special dispensation was needed for his burial in the Msida Bastion Cemetery because Vassalli had been a cleric in Minor Orders but never ordained, and had married whilst living in France.

Interest in the classical world was a hallmark of the intellectual and cultured circles of Europe at that time and Frere was very much part of that elite society. His own education was mainly based on the Classics. His house at Pietà probably contained one of the finest private libraries in Malta of the day, and it was a magnet to both local and foreign intellectuals. Indeed, he was a scholar in Greek and Latin literatures, as well as in Italian, French and Spanish. At the Villa in Pietà, he buried himself in his books, among the roses and vines of his garden, earning a reputation for being a man most famous for his erudition and knowledge of various languages and literature and for having a wonderful memory. He spent a good deal of time studying the Maltese and Hebrew languages and translating Greek authors. He made a fine translation of the medieval epic 'El Cid', and the metrical translations from Aristophanes, (The Acharnians, The Knights, The Frogs, and The Birds) are still considered definitive versions. In Academic circles he is much respected for his translations of Theognis Restilutus, The Iliad, The Odyssey, The Psalms of David, and an adaptation of Pulci's burlesque *Morgante Maggiore (The Monks and the Giants)* which influenced Byron's later poetry.

Frere and his wife were important figures of their day in the social and academic life of Malta, between 1822 and 1846, as we can judge by their impressive list of achievements. The Ladies' Charitable Society was founded in 1822 for the relief of the poor by providing them with clothing, straw for bedding, paying their house rents, and providing them with free medical attention by Dr. Giuseppe Stilon. The names of both Frere and his sister, Susan, appear in the list of subscribers to this Society. Another voluntary association, The Ladies of the Committee of the Soup Charity, of which Susan was a member, assisted the poor by providing them with free meals.

In September 1824, after a short time living in Malta, he was appointed by the British Governor, as President of a committee responsible for running the newly established House of Industry at Floriana, set up for the relief of the poor and unemployed. Apart from his official activities in this sphere, he contributed on his own initiative, to the welfare of the more needy of Maltese society. This generosity can be seen when he gave the largest sum by any individual to a fund raised for the relief of the dependents of eleven British and Maltese seaman and labourers, who had perished in the sinking of the schooner "*Meteor*" in February of 1834.

Education in Malta at this time was under review by the British Governor, Sir Frederick Ponsonby, who set up a Special Commission to inquire into the state of schooling in Malta. As a result, a General Council was formed by the University, with Frere as its first Chairman. He worked hard for the advancement of the Language Department of the University of Malta, and it was through his efforts that the first Chair of Maltese was established at the University.

He worked for the University until February 1833 when, aged 64, he resigned from his scholastic works, leaving behind him an impressive trail of studies showing how influential he had been in the encouragement of teaching of Hebrew, Greek, and the Maltese language itself. Today we can see a thriving Primary school, sited on part of the former gardens of the Villa, of which he would have been very proud.

After the death of his wife, in 1831, Frere arranged for her to be buried across the water at the Msida Bastion Cemetery, within his view from the Villa. Despite his family urging him to return to England, he remained in Malta, and it was at this point that the creation of the gardens began in earnest. His sister continued to live with him and their generous lives carried on.

During the terrible cholera epidemic of 1837, he gave financial assistance to thousands of Maltese people. His generosity was well known to all, and a crowd of lame, old and blind people used to gather in the evening at the door of the Villa to beg for alms, which were never refused. Those were times when the Maltese labourer depended for his livelihood on the expenditure of the British naval and military establishments in Malta. As the fate of business and military interests waned, so did the livelihood of the Maltese workers. At this time, emigration to Canada, America, and Australia was being encouraged as the main remedy against unemployment. Maltese labourers had been going to the Crimea and Gibraltar. Frere helped people to migrate to Tunis, Tripoli and Alexandria, where the Maltese language was more readily understood (being 80% Arabic in origin).

The death of his sister, Susan, in January 1839, affected him deeply. His wife had also died in January, and he later wrote that the month of January was a "most melancholy" one to him. He was himself to die in the month of January.

Frere was very interested in the Medical School, to which he donated a number of medical books. The Medical Association of his day appointed him an Honorary Member in 1843 in appreciation of his wide humanistic efforts. Again, it is highly suitable that St. Luke's Hospital, on Gwardamanga Hill, is sited so close to Villa Frere. It is sad to think that so few of its patients know anything about the famous gentleman who lived at the Villa just below, or the beautiful gardens on which the Hospital now stands.

Plate 15 ~ A stone bench

Chapter 5

Restoration of the Gardens by Edward Price

After the death of Frere in January 1846 and his burial in the Msida Bastion Cemetery, very little is known in detail about the Villa (apart from an advertisement in 1860 to let the 'magnificent house and stabling complete') until 1876, when Count Rosario Messina took the lease of the property.

Plate 16 Count and Countess Messina

The Messina family tree can be traced back several generations, including the macabre will, written in his own blood, by Count Giovanni Messina, in 1848 when he was imprisoned in Catanzaro during Garibaldi's uprising against the nobility. The opening greeting makes chilling reading – "My children, as I am expecting death shortly, listen to your father..." Giovanni Messina governed in Sicily, when it was divided into four parts at the beginning of the 19th century.

In 1876, his descendant, the merchant Count Rosario de Messina, of Bagnara, Calabria, with his wife, Maria de Ataliottis, came to live in Malta. She was the daughter of Nicholas de Ataliottis who lived in Valletta at N° 141, St. Christopher Street, later to become Palazzo Messina and which is today owned by the German Maltese Circle. The Messina family coat of arms can be seen inlaid in the marble floor of the Palazzo Messina.

Plate 17 Messina Coat of Arms

They had three sons and two daughters, who befriended my great-grandfather, the young Naval Officer Edward Price, on his many visits to Malta. The usual naval custom of making visiting ships welcome, was extended to him as a young midshipman. At these meetings, it is likely that he met his future wife, Giuseppina, but they were not to marry for another twelve years.

We have a fine record from him of life aboard in those days in his Journal that every midshipman has to write, even to this day. In May, 1872, he mentions swimming in Sliema Creek every morning, presumably because washing facilities were rather limited on board his ship, H.M.S. *Liffey*. His first recorded meeting with members of the Messina family is in his Journal entry for July 15th 1873, when he writes of "visiting the young Messina". Again, he mentions that he was visited by the Messina family on 20th October 1873 at the Quarantine Ground.

Due to frequent outbreaks of plague and disease, which were fatal in those days without modern medicines, a system of isolation for all passengers on arrival at the port was enforced. In Lazaretto Creek, a quarantine station had been constructed on Manoel Island, under the instructions of the Grand Master Lascaris in 1643, after two serious plagues. Visitors were incarcerated for a clean bill of health, for between 18 and 80 days, depending on where they had come from – hence quarantena/quarantine. To show how important the quarantine was, the yellow-uniformed quarantine guards, if caught sleeping on duty, were punished with a three year sentence as galley slaves. Many years later, Lord Byron referred to Malta as "this infernal oven" and spent 18 days confined in the lazaretto when coming home from Greece in 1811. Another sobering comment was made by Sir Walter Scott in 1831, when he remarked "It is unpleasant to be thought so very unclean and capable of poisoning a whole city". Names have a wonderful way of conveying history, and on sailing ships today, the lazaretto is a sealed locker at the stern of the ship.

A full account of the tragic burning of the Opera House in Valletta is to be found in Edward Price's journal, written on the morning of May 26th 1873, which gives a very immediate experience of the terrible accident.

"A very sad accident occurred last night which has put a stop to all our evenings' entertainments in the way of operas. About 9 o'clock last night, as we were smoking away quietly on deck, we saw a sudden blaze on shore and at once knew it was a fire, so of course I immediately collected together as many hands as we could spare out of the ship and took them ashore; taking with us tomahawks, fire buckets, ropes and a grapnel, in case they wanted any houses to be pulled down. We could not tell for certain from the ship what was on fire, some said the Club House, others the English Church, some the Opera House, but as soon as we landed I fell them in four deep and doubled up to where it was. To my horror it was the Opera House. When we got up to the House, I saw the Governor and two or three head swells holding a council of war. By this time, the whole of the interior was on fire, so we could do very little good. All we could do was to draw water from a well close by, and wet the houses all round to keep them as cool as possible. It was useless trying to save anything from inside as the place was one mass of flames. The great thing to do appeared to be to turn out the gas, which was soon done, leaving the town in darkness, with the exception of the light from the fire, which was as can be imagined quite sufficient. Luckily the outside of the building is of stone, so that the fire could not spread, but was kept inside. There were 90 tons of water kept on the top of the building in large tanks at the four corners. This, corners. This, immediately the fire broke out, was let out and the whole fell inside the building, but apparently did not the slightest good, and only made it worse and created a draught. After burning fiercely for about two hours, it gradually began to subside."

Although the Opera House was reconstructed four years after the accident, it was severely bombed in 1942, and to this day remains a ruin. It was designed by E.M. Barry, who was the architect of the Royal Opera House in London, and was built in 1866. Its design was unpopular, as it reflected the imperial nature of the British Empire. There are now, however, serious plans to rebuild it in conjunction with the Arts Centre at St James' Centre for Creativity.

Edward Price retired from the Royal Navy, as a Captain, in 1885. In his last ship, H.M.S. *Lively*, he was a member of the "Flying Squad", and one of the men

Plate 18 Giuseppina as a young bride

Plate 19 Marriage of Edward and Giuseppina Price

23

Plate 20 The Price Children in the Temple

world (being twice shipwrecked). On 24th August of the same year he married Giuseppina, Count Messina's daughter, which must have created a stir in the family circle by her marriage to an Englishman. They were married in Naples, by the Cardinal Archbishop of Naples, in the Private Chapel of his Palace.

The following year the newly married couple went to live at the house in Pietà, by now called Villa Frere, taking on the remaining 45 years of the lease from Count Rosario Messina. The Price family became a happy unit with three daughters, Mary, Dolores, and Josephine, and one son, Edward (Teddy).

Edward Price restored the neglected gardens with his creative enthusiasm, and the help of his Maltese gardeners.

Nichola   Mathew

Philomana

Plate 21 Maltese Gardeners

Features he added include a Japanese garden (complete with shrine and Buddha), an English Gnome garden and a Cactus garden.

Plates 22 a, b, & c : The Japanese Garden

The Japanese Garden was his pride and joy, which was overseen by a visiting Japanese Naval Officer.

Plate 23 The Japanese Garden

Plate 24 Edward Price with his Japanese advisor

Plate 25 English Gnome garden

Plate 26 Cactus garden

My mother, Anne, daughter of Dolores and her English husband, Francis Baxter (also an English Naval Officer), was a young girl of 8 when she stayed at Villa Frere on the occasion of her First Communion. There were grand afternoon receptions in the first floor salon, 'piano nobile', hosted by Edward and Giuseppina Price, where visiting friends were made welcome – to a child they seemed interminable, and she remembers escaping into the gardens or sitting up on the balconies of the Villa, overlooking the sea, where she could hear the exciting noises of life on the ships in the nearby harbour.

Plate 27 Dolores

Plate 28 Anne aged 8

Plate 29 (below) View from the Villa rooftop

The road in front of the Villa was once quiet, but is now a fast main road to Valletta.

Plate 30 Josephine and Dolores Price on the Upper Terrace

The views from the Villa have remained much the same and with a little imagination one can travel back in time to relive the elegant life that the Hookham Frere, Messina and Price families would have known.

Plate 31 Fishermen at Pietà

The life at the Villa was very sociable. The gardens continued to give pleasure to the family and all their visitors, including Queen Mary, and Prince George.

Plate 32 Queen Mary visits

Chapter 6

The Last Days of the Garden

Thankfully, the glory of the garden was recorded in an appreciative article in *Country Life*, in July 1930, before the devastation of the Second World War. By 1930 Edward Price's son, Teddy, now a Commander in the R.N., and to become the Chief Commissioner of the Scouts in 1936, was the only young member of the family still living in Malta.

Plate 33 Teddy Price

Plate 34 Teddy Price with Baden Powell

Edward Price, now 82, declined in health, and died in Malta on 28th June 1933. Giuseppina died six years later, aged 88 in 1939, at which point the Maltese Government took possession of Villa Frere.

Sadly the tradition of this Edwardian garden ended rather abruptly with World War II, and the gardens were severely bombed. Indeed, the whole Island suffered badly in what is referred to as the Second Great Siege. There have been various unsuccessful suggestions for the future of the Villa – amongst which were Nurses' Quarters, an Hotel, and construction of apartments. At present, the Villa is used for business purposes, and what remains of the fragmented garden is a wilderness. The Temple, the Wall with original gates still attached, and the Villa itself, are all that remains intact. There are several other old villas nearby in the same state of decay, and crying out for renovation so that future generations can enjoy their architectural history.

Plate 35 Captain and Mrs Edward Price

Plate 36 The Temple today

I have found the remembrance of a garden an intriguing piece of detective work, which has led into a simple study in social history. A garden is a reflection of its owner, and the gardens of Villa Frere would have been such an experience. Even today, with only photographs to show their detail, we can still appreciate the charm of what was undoubtedly one of Malta's most beautiful private gardens. The garden may be lost, but at least the old Villa still stands, with the name of a man in Malta's history, who should never be forgotten.

Plate 37 Gate and Turret near Hookham Frere Primary School today.

It is my own personal dream that the villa itself and that small portion of the original gardens which were not totally destroyed in the war, or subsequently built over, should be rescued and restored. Maybe one day this dream will be realised.

Chronology

1769	Birth of John Hookham Frere
1800	Last will of Giovanni Messina, in Catanzaro prison
1808	Frere sent to Spain as Plenipotentiary to the Central Junta
1816	Frere married Elizabeth Jemima, Dowager Countess of Errol
1820	Frere travelled by ship from England to Mediterranean with wife, sister, and wife's niece and settled in Malta
1821	Frere took 99 year lease of Villa
1824	The Ladies Malta Charitable Society formed
1831	Frere's wife died, buried in Msida Bastion Cemetery
1833	Frere retired from active University life, and began work on the Gardens
1835	Temple built. Statyra Lividostro married Capt. Hope, 7th Fusiliers, – Honoria Blake, niece of Lady Errol, married Lord Hamilton Chichester
1846	Death of John Hookham Frere aged 76
1851	Birth of Edward Price and Giuseppina Messina
1881	Death or Statyra Lividostro
1860	House unoccupied and garden overgrowing
1871	Publication of Frere's complete works, with memoir by his nephews
1876	Count Messina took over lease remaining (55 years)
1885	Marriage of Capt. Edward Price and Giuseppina Messina
1886	Capt. Price took over remaining 45 years of lease.
1888	Birth of Mary Price
1890	Birth of Edward Price (Teddy)
1891	Birth of Dolores (Dolly)
1894	Birth of Josephine (Baby)
1912	Queen Mary visited garden on her return from Indian Durbar.
1918	Dolores Price marries Francis Baxter

1930	St. Luke's Hospital building started. Article on garden in Country Life. Edward Price's son, Teddy, lived in Villa Messina until 1955
1933	Death of Capt. Price Government claims Villa Frere into the grounds of St. Luke's hospital
1936-55	Teddy Price serves as Chief Commissioner for the Scouts in Malta
1939	Death of Giuseppina Price
1940-43	War damage to gardens
1947	Villa Frere development proposal (Nurses Quarters) refused
1948	Villa leased to Clothing Factory
1957	Government Primary School opens in former gardens of Villa
1958	Capt. Teddy Price becomes the Manager of Phoenicia Hotel
1959	Proposal to build flats turned down by the Antiquities Committee
1960	James Hookham Frere, gt.gt.gt. nephew of Frere, lived at the Villa briefly
1968	Proposal to build an hotel on the site turned down
1972	Proposal to build an hotel on the site turned down again.